The Hallmarks Of Favour

God's Ways Of Blessing His People

Frederick Osei-Manu

The Hallmarks Of Favour

Scripture quotations are taken from the KING JAMES, of the Bible, unless otherwise. Emphasis within Scripture is the author's own.

ISBN: 978-0-359-75738-1

Published by Menorah House Publication

P.O. Box 17455, Accra

Telephone or Text: 0233(0)244735485

Email:fred18osei@hotmail.com

Editors: Charismata Editorial Services, Frederick Osei-Manu

Creative & Page Layout: Frederick Osei-Manu

Dedication

To Dr. Jerry Savelle and Dr. Mike Murdock: the men who made me fall in love with the message of "Favour. "

To you, the reader, who has taken time to read and be blessed by the revelations captured in this book.

Acknowledgements

To Dr. (Mrs) Anita Akosua Offeibea Osei-Manu and Mrs Emefa Mekpor who have been very instrumental in making this book become what it is today.

Contents

Translation Index

The author of this manuscript believes that the reading of the Bible from multiple translations helps one to get firm understanding of scriptures. It also makes it easy for one to convey his or her ideas in a very unique way. The author encourages the reader to actively collect more Bible translations to help the reader's walk with God.

An explanation of abbreviation, the translations used in this manuscript can be identified by the following codes:

AMP: Amplified Bible

ESV: English Standard Version

KJV: King James Version

MSG: The Message

NASB: New American Standard Bible

NIV: New International Version

TLB: The Living Bible

Prologue

***AND JESUS INCREASED** in wisdom and stature, and*
***IN FAVOUR WITH GOD AND MAN.** (Luke 2:52)*

There is something about favour. Jesus the greatest person of all time even needed favour to get him where He wanted to be in life and ministry. Favour is dimensional - that is why we have favour with God and the favour with men. God is greater than men. Therefore it is perfectly correct to say that the two favours mentioned are entirely different from one another. Let me put this in another way to help you appreciate it. Favour is both heavenly and earthly.

It is awesome to observe that Jesus had both heavenly and earthly favour working for Him. In this life, you will need both God and men for you to be able to accomplish your destiny. It is the ignorant morons who think they only need men, till they get to a place where they see the need for God. More so, those who only think men are not needed have twisted knowledge as to how things work here on the earth.

Bear in mind that God uses men as his channels of blessings in the earth. Never make a man your source, God is the only source you must rely on. Take a look at the wise men and the women in the scripture below and observe how they gave Jesus of their substance.

And when they were come into the house, they saw the young child with Mary his mother, and fell down, and worshipped him: and when they had opened their treasures, they presented unto him gifts; gold, and frankincense, and myrrh. (Matthew 2:11)

And certain women...Mary called Magdalene...And Joanna the wife of Chuza Herod's steward, and Susanna, and many others, which ministered unto him of their substance. (Luke 8:2-3)

You therefore need both heavenly and the earthly favour in all of your dealings. Often, people from all walks of life strive to gain the favours of their superiors. They will do anything to be accepted. They work hard, improve on their skills, and do everything they can to enable them gain the slighted opportunity to stand before or serve in a certain capacity before great people. This is naturally okay and there is nothing wrong with it.

However, there exist a favour that one gets before a person or a group that is not based or connected to anything the person has done. The person is just liked for who he is. This is the kind of favour with men that I would be talking about in this book.

In this book I also touched greatly on favour with God. This kind of favour is what makes divinity kick into or influence our humanity. Some also refer to it as when the supernatural comes into play in the naturalness of a people or on an event. Now just relax and enjoy this great read.

Introduction

Hard work cannot get you all you want but favour can get you more than you want. Is there anything like favour? Oh! yes, there is. I have seen people who were written-off but later became somebody because favour attended to them. I have seen people who were on the bottom of the ladder rise to the top of the ladder because favour moved on their behalf. The Bible even says it better.

I returned, and saw under the sun, that the race is not to the swift, nor the battle to the strong, neither yet bread to the wise, nor yet riches to men of understanding, NOR YET FAVOUR TO MEN OF SKILL; but time and chance happeneth to them all. (Ecclesiastes 9:11)

Blessed is the people that know the joyful sound: they shall walk, O LORD, in the light of thy countenance. In thy name shall they rejoice all the day: and in thy righteousness shall they be exalted. For thou art the glory of their strength: AND IN THY

FAVOUR OUR HORN SHALL BE EXALTED. (Psalms 89:15-17)

Favour can rewrite the stories of men and women; history indeed is full of these. Favour made it possible for:

- Noah and his family to be saved during the great flood (see Genesis 6:9-22; 7:1-24; 8:1-22).
- The barren and old stricken Abraham and Sarah to have a son of their own (see Genesis 17:19; 18:11; 21:2; Hebrews 11:11).
- Jacob and his family to be saved when the great famine came upon the earth (see Genesis 46-47).
- Joseph to be appointed a prime minister in Egypt (see Genesis 41:41).
- The cripple Mephibosheth to eat from the Kings table (see 2 Samuel 9:13).
- The orphan girl Esther to become a Queen (see Esther 2:1-17).
- Virgin Mary to conceive the Messiah, Jesus (see Luke 1: 26-35).

- The shepherd boy David became the most celebrated King in Israel (see 1 Samuel 16:1-13; 2 Samuel 5:1-5).
- Daniel to be preferred above all the wise men in Babylon (see Daniel 6:3).

Looking at all these people, what made it possible for them to be showcased and celebrated was by the force of favour. Favour will put you in a place where no man can put you.

Chapter 1
What Is Favour?

According to the Webster's Collegiate Thesaurus, favour could mean any of these words - respect, admiration, consideration, esteem, account, estimation, regard, blessing, approval, benediction, gift, present, compliment, aid, assistance, help, backing, encouragement, support, a special privilege, courtesy, dispensation, indulgence, kindness, service, approbate, countenance, endorse, appreciate, prize, value, pamper, accommodate, convenience, feature, encourage, cooperation, fortunate, advantage and simulate.

I decided to also research on what others have said about favour. It means - preferential treatment, kind act, a token of goodwill and exceptional regard. It is also important we take a look at how the word 'favour' is used in the Bible. From the Strong's Hebrew lexicon ' favour' could mean any of the following—beauty, precious, pleasant, gracious, bestow, gift, best, better, skilful, enjoy, desire, delight, greet, move, successful, benefit, health, welfare, prosperity, wealth, health, most, merry, joyful, wish, bountiful, cheerful, happy, sweet, ready, delight in, goodness, have pleasure, whosoever would, willing, supplication, entreat, fair, pleased with, kindness to an inferior, to bend or stoop in, the eye of the landscape, right forth, well seen, well said, be accepted, benefit, honourable, set affection, pardon, voluntary will, peace, salute, safe, rest, friendly, joy liberality and divine influence upon the heart .

Time will not permit me to look into each and every synonym used for the word "favour". I believe you would agree with me that when the word 'favour' is used by men and women, it produces marvellous results. Imagine you were talking with somebody and used the words *"Can you do me a favour?"*, it changes the way the conversation goes. In other words, you are telling the person, let my wish be your command.

When favour goes before anyone, you certainly know that good things are awaiting such a fellow.

Favour can rewrite the stories of people. It can change the position and status of people.

It is on this note that I want to write on 'favour'. If there is any man who walked the earth and enjoyed so much favour it was Jesus Christ. His birth was on the platform of favour. Till date, he is the only one born of a virgin.

The announcement of the birth of Jesus by the angel and the rest of the host was a proclamation of favour to the whole human race. You take a look at the words the angels spoke.

And the angel said unto them, FEAR NOT: FOR, BEHOLD, I BRING YOU GOOD TIDINGS OF GREAT JOY, WHICH SHALL BE TO ALL PEOPLE. For unto you is born this day in the city of David a Saviour, which is Christ the Lord...And suddenly there was with the angel a multitude of the heavenly host praising God, and saying, Glory to God in the highest, AND ON EARTH PEACE, GOOD WILL TOWARD MEN. (Luke 2:10, 11, 13, 14)

Think about the kind of words spoken above; it makes me feel elated. Imagine you open the door of your house and you are met by an exceeding, high, great, large, loud sound of joy by a crowd of happy people. You begin to wonder what you have done to deserve this kind of welcome. The truth is that it is not based on anything you have done but what God has done for you.

This is the good news God has always intended for you to hear in every situation in your life. That is what the angels were making known on that fateful day. If this is not favour, then tell me what it is?

End Note

Strong's Concordance with Hebrew and Greek Lexicon - EliYah *http://www.eliyah.com/cgi-bin/strongs.cgi?file=hebrewlexicon&isindex=favour*

Chapter 2

How To Trigger Favour

Though we all know favour is not something we qualify to receive, it has certain codes by which it works. These codes are inbuilt into the universe by God and it functions all the time. Once anyone adheres to this code, favour can be activated. I have found a few of these codes in the Bible.

#1. Love For God

My son, forget not my law; but let thine heart keep my commandments: For length of days, and long life, and peace, shall they add to thee. Let not mercy and truth forsake thee: bind them about thy neck; write them upon the table of thine heart: So shalt thou find favour and good understanding in the sight of God and man. (Proverbs 3:1-4)

When a person has a heart for God, he or she is ready for the best of God. When two people are in love there is no boundary to how one showers the other with gifts. It is the same when one's heart is knit with that of God; the flow of favour cannot be stopped.

#2. Love For Righteousness

Thou hast loved righteousness, and hated iniquity; therefore God, even thy God, hath anointed thee with the oil of gladness above thy fellows. (Hebrews 1:9)

To love light is to dislike darkness. To love righteousness is to abhor sin. This is one thing that placed Jesus over and above any of contemporaries. Do you desire an enviable success in life and ministry; then follow this same roadmap.

#3. Sowing The Right Seeds

Be not deceived; God is not mocked: for whatsoever a man soweth, that shall he also reap. (Galatians 6:7)

A gift from your hand into somebody's life can create cycles of favour for you. A choice word can direct the attention of your boss towards you. Giving somebody a helping hand can open a room for you.

#4. Delighting In Wisdom

Blessed is the man that heareth me, watching daily at my gates, waiting at the posts of my doors. For whoso findeth me findeth life, and shall obtain favour of the LORD. (Proverbs 8:34-35)

Those who take interest in searching for wisdom are eligible to gain God's favour. It is wisdom that makes the simple wise. A wise man or woman knows how to order his or her steps in life.

Wise people usually know what to say and not say; so they are able to attract the favour of people in any environment. The wise can actually access impossible doors because they know which key to use.

Wisdom is said to be applied knowledge. I have observed that among men, the one who has vast knowledge and knows what he or she is about is usually chosen above the person whose knowledge is limited.

#5. A Good Heart

A good man obtaineth favour of the LORD: but a man of wicked devices will he condemn. A man shall not be established by wickedness: but the root of the righteous shall not be moved. (Proverbs 12:2-3)

Decide to be a good person with a good heart towards all humans and favour will gravitate in your direction. Never allow the callous things that stream around this world to affect your heart.

As a young boy, my parents told me that "the best gift you can give to people is your good heart." As an adult, I perfectly see the sense in this statement. When you do good to others, you are indirectly helping yourself. The result of your acts of kindness is joy and procured favour waiting to show in your life later.

There is another lesson I want you to get. When you make up your mind to do good to those around, do not look at some of the negative attitudes people put up. When you look at men as men; you may never do any good any more.

It was Albert Einstein who once said "few are those who see with their own eyes and feel with their own hearts. Indeed, only a few people turn their hearts towards the pains and hurts of others.

I have heard people over and over again say "I have not finished solving my problems so why should I bother to help others." The truth is that we all need or will somebody at one point or the other. This is because problems are part of the human life; only the dead are problem-free. I admonish that we should carry a good heart around; for it is a gateway to touching lives.

#6. The Power Of Meditation

The one thing I want from God, the thing I seek most of all, is the privilege of meditating in his Temple, living in his presence every day of my life, delighting in his incomparable perfections and glory. (Psalms 27:4, TLB)

Today, meditation has come to the limelight in the Western world. Unfortunately, the majority of the meditation has been channelled to the wrong source instead of God. The shepherd boy David who later became king in Israel paid great attention to meditation.

Meditation is simply the contemplations of thoughts, words, pictures, things and persons. When we talk about meditation we are simply referring to a concentrated focus. What you give attention to has the right to manifest in your life and world.

This book of the law shall not depart out of thy mouth; but thou shalt meditate therein day and night, that thou mayest observe to do according to all that is written therein: for then thou shalt make thy way prosperous, and then thou shalt have good success. (Joshua 1:8)

When your mind is stayed on God and on his Word, you give yourself the right to interact with something higher than you. This kind of delighting and reflections puts you in a position to attract God's favour.

God's favour can shift your world into an entirely different orbit. I was carried away when I saw the benefits of meditation from the Hebrew meanings of the words - prosperous and good success. Prosperous means - to push forward, break out, come mightily, go over, be good, be meet and be profitable. Good success means - wisdom, wise, skill, intelligent, expert, prudent, consider, circumspect and guide wittingly. Just these words would put you on top in any field.

#7. Association

And Lot also, which went with Abram, had flocks, and herds, and tents. (Genesis 13:5)

Lot became rich because he followed Abram, whose name later became Abraham. It is Abraham we know who originally had the blessing but we also see its effect on Lot's life. What was on Abraham out flowed into Lot's life. Favour is very contagious. This is why it is important to hang out with the right person and the right crowd.

#8.Giving

And Noah builded an altar unto the LORD; and took of every clean beast, and of every clean fowl, and

offered burnt offerings on the altar. And the LORD smelled a sweet savour; and the LORD said in his heart, I will not again curse the ground any more for man's sake; for the imagination of man's heart is evil from his youth; neither will I again smite any more every thing living, as I have done. While the earth remaineth, seedtime and harvest, and cold and heat, and summer and winter, and day and night shall not cease. (Genesis 8:20-22)

Giving can move the Heavens in your favour. It was Noah's giving that caught God's attention after the flood. God smelt the offering and was pleased with what Noah had done. We give out of love and reverence of God and not to buy His favour. Those who give with the notion of buying God's favour have missed the essence of giving. God is too big to be bought with an offering. Actually, God owns everything; there is no need to coax him.

Noah gave his offering to God as an act of worship and God was moved to speak with Noah on a level He had not done before. God told Noah that because of his offering, He pledges not to deal with men in that manner again. Then God went ahead to hand a revelation concerning seedtime and harvest to Noah.

#9. Worship

And the ark of the LORD continued in the house of Obededom the Gittite three months: and the LORD blessed Obededom, and all his household. And it was told king David, saying, The LORD hath blessed the house of Obededom, and all that pertaineth unto him, because of the ark of God. So David went and brought up the ark of God from the house of Obededom into the city of David with gladness. (2 Samuel 6:11-12)

Within three months a significant thing began to take place in Obededom's life and household because he hosted the ark of God. Worship is what Obededom gave on his part to God as his service to Him. The whole duty of man revolves around worship so once a man taps into it with the right heart, God is obliged to honour such a person.

It is worship that won King David the place as a man after God's own heart. When David heard of the good Obededom was enjoying, he wanted the whole nation of Israel to also experience it; so he went to fetch the ark of God to the city of David. A man or woman who knows how to worship and can really play the strings and chords in the heart of God is special to God. Worship will gain you favour any day.

#10. Prayer & Fasting

Go, gather together all the Jews that are present in Shushan, and fast ye for me, and neither eat nor drink three days, night or day: I also and my maidens will fast likewise; and so will I go in unto the king, which is not according to the law: and if I perish, I perish. (Esther 4:16)

Fasting simply means staying away from food for a period. The sole purpose of fasting is to give oneself room to engage God. When we fast we humble ourselves to receive the blessings and favour of God. The Jews were faced with a king's decree of mass wiping of their generation. This was engineered through the wicked plot of Haman, all because one Mordecai will not bow to him.

Mordecai encouraged all Jews including Queen Esther to fast to avert this wicked plan of Haman. On a normal day, no man or woman goes before the King until the King calls for the person. This fasting and prayers, however, gave Queen Esther such favour before King Ahasuerus; to such an extent that the palace protocol was not observed.

All the king's servants, and the people of the king's provinces, do know, that whosoever, whether man or woman, shall come unto the king into the inner court, who is not called, there is one law of his to put him to death, except such to whom the king shall hold out the golden sceptre, that he may live: but I have not been called to come in unto the king these thirty days. (Esther 4:11)

Queen Esther discloses that Haman seeks her life and that of her people. The king was agitated knowing that his hands have been twisted to take the very life of his wife. The long and short of the story is that Haman was hanged.

And it was so, when the king saw Esther the queen standing in the court, that she obtained favour in his

sight: and the king held out to Esther the golden sceptre that was in his hand. So Esther drew near, and touched the top of the sceptre. (Esther 5:2)

End Note

Heart Quotes | Best Famous Quotations About Heart –Ranker

https://www.ranker.com/list/notable-and-famous-heart-quotes/reference

Chapter 3

Declaration Of Favour

At the time of writing this book, the current government of Ghana had launched a free Senior High School (SHS) program. This is good news for the citizens, especially for the youth and parents.

I brought this up to make a certain remark. Come to think of it, if men can make powerful declarations, how much more God's declaration of favour. God's declaration of favour cannot be matched.

The Spirit of the Lord GOD is upon me; because the LORD hath anointed me to preach good tidings unto the meek; he hath sent me to bind up the brokenhearted, to proclaim liberty to the captives, and the opening of the prison to them that are bound; To PROCLAIM THE ACCEPTABLE YEAR OF THE LORD[THE YEAR OF THE LORD'S FAVOUR], and the day of vengeance of our God; to comfort all that mourn; To appoint unto them that mourn in Zion, to give unto them beauty for ashes, the oil of

joy for mourning, the garment of praise for the spirit of heaviness; that they might be called trees of righteousness, the planting of the LORD, that he might be glorified. And they shall build the old wastes, they shall raise up the former desolations, and they shall repair the waste cities, the desolations of many generations. And strangers shall stand and feed your flocks, and the sons of the alien shall be your plowmen and your vinedressers. **(Isaiah 61:1-5 *with the author's insertion*)**

Once a declaration is gone forth, it is required of you to take advantage of it. In one of Kenneth Hagin Senior's books, he tells the story of a man who was on board of a ship but never enjoyed the free food served at the restaurants. One of the days he was asked by another person; why he does not join them when it is time for eating.

The man answers this fellow – I don't have money to buy from the restaurant. The fellow tells this man, you have already paid for it. How? He asked. The man answered – It is part of the ticket that guaranteed your place on the ship. This man's ignorance made him chew biscuits when there was tantalizing food all the while for him.

How many of us go through life like this. Bear in mind, all things are yours including God's declaration of favour. Any time I think about how Israel became rich and powerful when they were leaving Egypt; I just think of favour. The Bible says it all.

Tell the people that men and women alike are to ask their neighbours for articles of silver and gold. THE LORD MADE THE EGYPTIANS FAVOURABLY DISPOSED TOWARD THE PEOPLE, and Moses himself was highly regarded in Egypt by Pharaoh's officials and by the people. (Exodus 11:2-3, NIV)

And the children of Israel did according to the word of Moses, and they borrowed of the Egyptians jewels of silver, and jewels of gold, and raiment: AND THE LORD GAVE THE PEOPLE FAVOUR IN THE SIGHT OF THE EGYPTIANS, SO THAT THEY LENT UNTO THEM SUCH THINGS AS THEY REQUIRED. And they spoiled the Egyptians. (Exodus 12:35, 36)

In a single day, slaves became part of the upper echelon of Egypt. Wealth (raiment, jewels of silver and gold) moved hands from the Egyptians to the

Jews by the force of favour. Favour can alter positions. The Egyptians felt liable to make provisions available to the Jews under strange circumstances. Who in his normal mind will give out his treasured possession to somebody who is not within his or her golden circle? The Jews were not close to Egyptians by relation but they 'got all that mattered in Egypt.' Indeed, *such things as they required* the Egyptians willingly handed over to the Jews. The wealth of Egypt was gone in a day. What a day this must be. This took place about 3,500 years ago.

Set Time

Thou shalt arise, and have mercy upon Zion: FOR THE TIME TO FAVOUR HER, YEA, THE SET TIME, IS COME. For thy servants take pleasure in her stones, and favour the dust thereof. (Psalms 102:13, 14)

According to the Talmud (i.e. a collection of Jewish traditional ceremonial and civil law or simply means "instruction"), for 240 years 600,000 Jew slaves were subjected to unpaid labour by the Egyptians. So by the claims of justice from God's end, the way to pay back Israel was by a set time of favour. Once the time of favour was set, God told Moses to let the Jews rush in to ask Egyptians for their resources. If any of the Jews had gone before this set time they would have gone empty-handed.

One of God's ways of rewarding or blessing His people is through the power of favour. In our time, because we have fixed our heart on the prosperity of Zion (the Church) with our time, effort and money – it provokes God to take action on our behalf.

Favour Impacts Every Realm Of Life

A jubilee shall that fiftieth year be unto you: ye shall not sow, neither reap that which groweth of itself in it, nor gather the grapes in it of thy vine undressed. For it is the jubilee; it shall be holy unto you: ye shall eat the increase thereof out of the field. (Leviticus 25:11, 12)

The laws of the earth are such that what you sow, you reap. Without one sowing, reaping is impossible. This principle and thought are perfectly welcome in the realm of men. It is therefore surprising when favour moves a man, a woman or a people above the norm for them to enjoy what they never sowed. We usually call this a miracle.

Favour makes sufficient increase possible. When you read the passage above carefully you will realise that God instructed the nation of Israel to only feed on what was in the field. They needed not to exert their labour (like ploughing and sowing) to make something to happen so they could eat.

Favour introduces jubilee. According to Matthew Henry's Commentary, in the year of jubilee, all properties and all liberties are restored. All debts are cancelled and everyone gets a fresh start to life. Favour always provokes new seasons and times in the life of men (women inclusive).

End Notes

Kenneth Hagin Snr.

An Embarrassment Of Riches

https://people.ucalgary.ca/~elsegal/Shokel/M06Passover_Spoils.html

Matthew Henry's Commentary On The Whole Bible Complete And Unabridged

An Exposition, With Practical Observations, Of Third Book of Moses, Called Leviticus, pg182

Talmud | Define Talmud at Dictionary.com

https://www.dictionary.com/browse/talmud

Chapter 4
To Be Well-Spoken Of

But the LORD was with Joseph, and shewed him mercy, and gave him favour in the sight of the keeper of the prison. And the keeper of the prison committed to Joseph's hand all the prisoners that were in the prison; and whatsoever they did there, he was the doer of it. The keeper of the prison looked not to anything that was under his hand; because the LORD was with him, and that which he did, the LORD made it to prosper. (Genesis 39:21-23)

When Joseph was thrown into prison, one would have thought that would be his end. He was serving a time in prison for an offence he never committed. However, this was not the case, God was on Joseph's side and he the Almighty made the prison guard take another look of who Joseph was. The prison guard favoured Joseph and had him become a supervisor over his colleagues. All that moved and went on in the prison was now Joseph's responsibility. Remember this, favour never knows limitation.

The whole story has it that when Joseph was in prison he had an opportunity to interpret dreams for two prisoners who happen to be Pharaoh's butler and baker. The butler was reinstated and baker killed. Joseph asked the butler to remember him when he is freed. It is often said, *"out of sight out of mind."* Two years passed before the butler remembered him.

Pharaoh was wroth with his servants, and put me in ward in the captain of the guard's house, both me and the chief baker: And we dreamed a dream in one night, I and he; we dreamed each man according to the interpretation of his dream. And there was there with us a young man, an Hebrew, servant to the captain of the guard; and we told him, and he interpreted to us our dreams; to each man according to his dream he did interpret. And it came to pass, as he interpreted to us, so it was; me he restored unto mine office, and him he hanged. Then Pharaoh sent and called Joseph, and they brought him hastily out of the dungeon: and he shaved himself, and changed his raiment, and came in unto Pharaoh. (Genesis 41:10-14)

One thing I have realised about people is that they have a short memory and it usually takes something special to trigger a remembrance. Pharaoh had a dream and sought for interpretation, it was only then that the butler remembered Joseph. The butler spoke well of Joseph to Pharaoh; that he is the man gifted to interpret his dream.

You need to appreciate that for one to cross carpets to access great people and great places, he or she must be well-spoken of. This is exactly what took place. Joseph was fetched from prison, his garment was changed and clean shaved to enable him to stand before Pharaoh.

WELL-SPOKEN WORDS BRING SATISFACTION; well-done work has its own reward. (Proverbs 12:14, MSG)

God chose to use the key of being well-spoken of to bring Joseph to a place of prominence. I am wondering what would be going through the mind of Joseph as he stood before Pharaoh (the most powerful leader) in his age. I think he was humbled. Pharaoh told Joseph his dream. Joseph then interprets the dream and it sounded good to Pharaoh.

It is amazing to know that the few words of the butler led to a change Joseph's location and position in life in a season he least expected. This must be God at work here. After, Joseph went on to become the second most influential person in Egypt.

Let me move on to talk about another person who was also well-spoken of- Demetrius. Little is known about the history of Demetrius but one thing that stands out is that he had a good report before people and God.

DEMETRIUS IS WELL SPOKEN OF BY EVERYONE - and even by the truth itself. We also speak well of him, and you know that our testimony is true. (3 John 1:12, NIV)

Matthew Henry's Commentary talks about Demetrius in this manner - *"But here his name will live. A name in the gospel, a fame in the churches, is better than that of sons and daughters."* I recall listening to Dr Mike Murdock as he talked about how Rev. Oral Roberts commended him to become the 27th board member of the Charismatic Bible Fellowship. As at that time, Dr

Murdock was not as well-known as the other great men on the board. Do you know that because of the recommendation of Rev. Roberts, great doors began to open for Dr Murdock? Do you know that your fraternity is what creates the golden circles of favour in your world?

End Notes

Matthew Henry's Commentary On The Whole Bible Complete And Unabridged
An Exposition, With Practical Observations, Of the Third Epistle of John, pg 2459

Dr Mike Murdock
8 Things That Create Prosperity, posted on YouTube on December 3, 2016

Chapter 5
Suspending Natural Laws

Then spake Joshua to the LORD in the day when the LORD delivered up the Amorites before the children of Israel, and he said in the sight of Israel, SUN, STAND THOU STILL UPON GIBEON; AND THOU, MOON, IN THE VALLEY OF AJALON. AND THE SUN STOOD STILL, AND THE MOON STAYED, until the people had avenged themselves upon their enemies. Is not this written in the book of Jasher? SO THE SUN STOOD STILL IN THE MIDST OF HEAVEN, AND HASTED NOT TO GO DOWN ABOUT A WHOLE DAY. And there was no day like that before it or after it, that the LORD hearkened unto the voice of a man: for the LORD fought for Israel. (Joshua 10:12-14)

It will only take favour with God to be able to suspend the natural laws of creation. How the sun and other planets evolve is not in the control of men but God. In other words, the planetary system is independent of the activities of men.

Joshua an intern of Moses, who later became the leader of Israel asked God to do the unusual so they can gain victory over the enemies. The prayer or request of Joshua demanded that the day be lengthened. This demanded that instead of the earth taking 24 hours to complete a full rotation, it took 48 hours. The earth's speed of movement on its axis was slowed down because the sun and moon were made to stay still by the supernatural hand of God.

I want you to take note of the following things I am about to put across. Sun standing still in the Hebrew language means "sun - cease acting, stop working, be silent, rest, tarry and wait". And the moon staying still in the Hebrew language would mean "moon – abide, dwell, remain and be employed." These two events would only take a miraculous event to occur. Indeed, God is in charge of the Cosmos.

Some scientists believe that the moon stood between the sun and the earth causing an eclipse to occur. The sun withdrew its rays and darkness covered the earth just at the voice of a man. Prior to this time, the army of Israel had the upper hand in the battle and they needed extra time to alienate their enemies. God was actively fighting for Israel because Heaven was releasing great stones and hailstones against the Amorites (see Joshua 10:11). Israel's army defeated the five armies in this particular battle.

Never in the history of men have God stopped the sun and moon at a man's prayers. However because Israel had favour with God, He altered heavenly proceedings and protocols to grant Joshua his request. I went all this way to explain the text so you will appreciate the great victory God gave Joshua and the people of Israel.

Let me quickly touch on how Elisha moved into something mega than he had ever thought about.

He took up also the mantle of Elijah that fell from him, and went back, and stood by the bank of Jordan; And he took the mantle of Elijah that fell from him, and smote the waters, and said, Where is the LORD God of Elijah? and when he also had smitten the waters, they parted hither and thither: and Elisha went over. **(2 Kings 2:13, 14)**

Elisha had followed closely his mentor and spiritual father (Elijah) and now the time had come for him to pick the mantle of this great prophet. He picks up the mantle and does exactly what he saw Elijah do before they went over the Jordan.

He smote the river with Elijah's mantle and went over to the side of the river. Elisha saw a miracle right before his eyes. Elisha's life and ministry were changed instantly. When something of this sort happens, you should know that the force of favour is at work. Favour provokes the supernatural to happen.

A New Rising Generation

And we all, who with unveiled faces contemplate [reflect, behold] the Lord's glory, are being transformed into his image with ever-increasing glory, which comes from the Lord, who is the Spirit. (2 Corinthians 3:18, NIV)

There is a new generation of believers rising up that would do exceedingly great things in these last days that would make the world look up to God. As these believers behold the face of God more intently and passionately, they will come to a place where the glory of God would manifest on certain levels that would override natural laws. In the glory of God, there is favour and the vice versa is perfectly true. Bear in mind that favour can alter the natural laws of this earth. So when God sheds His favour on you, expect something marvellous to take place in your life.

End Notes

Joshua Commanded The Sun And Moon To Stand Still… Not The Earth
http://robschannel.com/joshua-commanded-the-sun-and-moon-to-stand-still-not-the-earth

Don Stewart | Did The Sun Actually Stand Still In Joshua's Long Day? - Blue Letter Bible
https://www.blueletterbible.org/faq/don_stewart/don_stewart_625.cfm

Chapter 6

Kinds Of Favour

The two main kinds of favour are - one from God and one from man. You really need both favours to help you get to where God wants you to get to. In this chapter, you will see how these two kinds of favour affected men and even shaped the course of history.

How Favour Saved A Man And His Family

But Noah found grace in the eyes of the LORD. (Genesis 6:8)

God intended to bring a flood on the earth and chose a man by name Noah to warn people of the impending judgement. The people of the day rejected Noah's warning. The flood eventually came upon the earth but for Noah and his family, they were saved by the ark which God made him build.

The ark became the way of escape for this man and his family when the heavy rains came upon the earth. It is favour that prevented Noah's family from suffering what every other family experienced.

Favour Provokes Uncommon Harvest

And I will make of you a great nation, and I will bless you [with abundant increase of favors] and make your name famous and distinguished, and you will be a blessing [dispensing good to others]. (Genesis 12:2, AMP)

***Then Isaac sowed in that land, and received in the same year an hundredfold: and the LORD blessed him.* (Genesis 26:12)**

There was a heavy drought that was prevailing in Isaac's day. In the middle of this drought, God instructed Isaac to sow seeds in his fields. He promptly obeyed God and reaped a hundredfold harvest.

Favour Has A Way Of Releasing Strange Help

And the servant ran to meet her, and said, Let me, I pray thee, drink a little water of thy pitcher. And she

said, Drink, my lord: and she hasted, and let down her pitcher upon her hand, and gave him drink. And when she had done giving him drink, she said, I will draw water for thy camels also, until they have done drinking. And she hasted, and emptied her pitcher into the trough, and ran again unto the well to draw water, and drew for all his camels. (Genesis 24:17-20)

Eliezer of Damascus, a steward of Abraham embarks on a journey to find a wife for his master's son—Isaac. While on the journey he prays that God would show him good speed and kindness for his mission (see Genesis 24:12). Not long after, Rebekah appears from nowhere to offer him kindness. This gorgeous lady offered him water and went ahead to provide water for his camels. Indeed she went out of her way to offer Eliezer such a strange help. Remember that Eliezer was a stranger in town and had done nothing to deserve this kind gesture. Nonetheless, favour was 'the angel' that made this happening to come in place.

Favour Makes Struggles Come To An End

And he removed from thence, and digged another well, and FOR THAT THEY STROVE NOT: and he called the name of it Rehoboth; and he said, For now, the LORD hath made room for us, and we shall be fruitful in the land. (Genesis 26:22)

The Philistines always contended with the servants of Isaac any time they found a well. Business was not too pleasant for Isaac's men. This meant that they had to find water from other sources for the animals in their care.

But a day came when they found a new well and Philistines could not claim ownership over it. At last, these servants would not need to go through tough times of finding water any more. The struggle with the Philistines was now over. Favour terminated this evil that was proceeding all the time between them and the Philistines. There is favour available for you to end the current toiling you are probably experiencing.

Favour Is The Architect Of Sweet Discoveries

And he removed from thence, and DIGGED ANOTHER WELL, and for that, they strove not: and he called the name of it Rehoboth; and he said, For now, the LORD hath made room for us, and we shall be fruitful in the land. (Genesis 26:22)

Water is a precious commodity for any farmer. The servants of Isaac discovered a well and knew God had established their farming business. They also knew they would certainly flourish like never before.

A discovery in any field is likely to get the attention of many. Today when one gets a niche or discover a breakthrough in business, the world goes after them. The favour of God can cause you to see and have things that you would have never had before.

Favour Stirs Up Increase And Growth

And they, continuing daily with one accord in the temple, and breaking bread from house to house, did

eat their meat with gladness and singleness of heart, Praising God, and having favour with all the people. And the Lord added to the church daily such as should be saved. (Acts 2:46, 47)

To have a thriving ministry, business and family; one will need the favour of God and men. To experience increase and growth in ministry, in particular, does not come automatically. Having done ministry for years, I know that you can invite as many people as possible for a program or a meeting and the feedback after will not be convincing.

Surprisingly, in the early church, this was not the outcome. For them, they were experiencing daily additions to their number. Indeed the early church had favour before the people.

How Drought Was Turned Into Overflow

But I tell you of a truth, many widows were in Israel in the days of Elias, when the heaven was shut up three years and six months, when great famine was

throughout all the land; But unto none of them was Elias sent, save unto Sarepta, a city of Sidon, unto a woman that was a widow. (Luke 4:25, 26)

Arise, get thee to Zarephath, which belongeth to Zidon, and dwell there: behold, I have commanded a widow woman there to sustain thee...For thus saith the LORD God of Israel, The barrel of meal shall not waste, neither shall the cruse of oil fail, until the day that the LORD sendeth rain upon the earth. And she went and did according to the saying of Elijah: and she, and he, and her house did eat many days. And the barrel of meal wasted not, neither did the cruse of oil fail, according to the word of the LORD, which he spake by Elijah. (1 Kings 17:9, 14-16)

A widow who did not know where her meals would come from after her last meal was supernatural sustained by God's act of favour of sending Elijah to her. It does not make sense that one would use the same barrel of meal and cruse of oil for two and half years. But this is what exactly took place in her house. What a spectacle this must be for her and the son.

Favour brought such a mighty prophet as Elijah into her life and house. It must be favour that allowed her to even host Elijah. Over the years of having observed prophets, I realised they just don't act anyhow. More so, prophets do not go about asking people for meals. Often than not they must align with what God is doing. However, favour made Elijah break certain prophetic protocols all in the process of preserving this woman and her son. Elijah a Jew had to cross carpets to stay with a Gentile woman for two and a half years.

When God leads a prophet to a place and a person, it means something big and unusual is about taking place. In the midst of drought, this widow was enjoying plenty. Tell me if this is not favour.

Favour Can Turn Tables Around

And the king loved Esther above all the women, and she obtained grace and favour in his sight more than all the virgins; so that he set the royal crown upon her head, and made her queen instead of Vashti. Then the king made a great feast unto all his princes and

his servants, even Esther's feast; and he made a release to the provinces, and gave gifts, according to the state of the king. (Esther 2:17-18)

Queen Vashti's position was made vacant and Esther came into her stead. Esther's background naturally did not allow her to wear the crown but favour got her to become the king's wife.

God's favour has such power in turning the tables to your honour. Within a day Esther's address was changed. Do you know that her connections, sitting place, dresses and the kind of meals were upgraded?

In my mind's eye, I wonder how Esther felt- probably shocked, mesmerized, in cloud nine, happy etc. I tell you this truth; favour can amaze you so much that you will find it difficult to get words to describe the happenings.

Favour Makes One Preferred Over Another

As it is written, Jacob have I loved, but Esau have I hated. What shall we say then? Is there unrighteousness with God? God forbid. (Romans 9:13, 14)

God is not partial in nature. Before time will unfold, before the birth of these boys (Esau and Jacob), God had already made His choice. Jacob did nothing to deserve why God selected him above his brother Esau.

In the natural, the eldest brother usually gets the birthright and the blessing. But something dramatic would take place between these boys to force their hands to change position. Though you may say Jacob played cleverly to get birthright from Esau, God had a hand in it. Again you may say that Rachael coaching Jacob made it possible for him to snatch the blessing from Esau. Keep in mind that God had already put Jacob above Esau and with time this was about to play out.

Favour Makes People Hold You In High Esteem

My dove, my undefiled is but one; she is the only one of her mother, she is the choice one of her that bare her. The daughters saw her, and blessed her; yea, the queens and the concubines, and they praised her. (Song of Solomon 6:9)

To stand out among a thousand women and be liked by these same women takes favour. The Shunnamite lady was the favourite of her siblings. And when it came to King Solomon, she was the darling of his heart.

When you are held in high esteem, people shower blessings and praises on you. This was the kind of experience the Shunnamite woman had on a daily basis. I pray that in your next experience, the God of favour would be the One behind it and cause people to highly esteem you.

When Favour Plays Out, We All Get Freaked Out

For the seed shall be prosperous; the vine shall give her fruit, and the ground shall give her increase, and the heavens shall give their dew; and I will cause the remnant of this people to possess all these things. And it shall come to pass, that as ye were a curse among the heathen, O house of Judah, and the house of Israel; so will I save you, and ye shall be a

blessing: fear not, but let your hands be strong. (Zechariah 8:12, 13)

Every farmer values seeds and fruits; they know their livelihood depends on it. Where a farmer does everything but does not see the kind of harvest wanted, it becomes very frustrating. But where the farmer goes into his or her field and sees a harvest beyond his or her expectation, they really get freaked out. They know the role of heaven in what they see.

When heaven moves over the life of a person, they experience what we call "favour". It is not surprising that the nation Israel with the smallest population in the world was picked by God as a choice vine among other nations. The heathen nations could not understand this but there was nothing they could do about it. Israel was chosen above the others by the favour of God and to be blessed by Him.

Supernatural Inclusion

For if the firstfruit [talking about the Jews] be holy, the lump is also holy: and if the root be holy, so are the branches [referring to the Gentiles]. And if some of

the branches be broken off, and thou, being a wild olive tree, wert graffed [were grafted] in among them, and with them partakest of the root and fatness of the olive tree. (Romans 11:16, 17 with the author's insertion)

Gentiles or heathen nations were in time past seen as an outcast before God. Amazingly, after the resurrection of Jesus, they were grafted into the commonwealth of Israel. So then the blessing of Abraham has now been made available to them; just as the Jews.

Favour makes supernatural inclusion possible. Do you know that favour never takes into account your shortcomings, failures and weakness? When favour is at work, it just goes ahead to override all these things and makes one qualified and accepted.

Chapter 7

Out Of The Blue

And strangers shall stand and feed your flocks, and the sons of the alien shall be your plowmen and your vinedressers. (Isaiah 61:5)

We all love surprises. Anytime my wife says she has a surprise for the children their attention get aroused. A surprise is simply an out of the blue manifestation. We are used to getting things done for us by ourselves, family and friends. Nevertheless, when a stranger or a foreigner does something for us we get surprised. Favour is what compels strangers or foreigners to be a blessing to us.

Dr. Jerry Savelle was once moved by Holy Spirit to write these words *"Begin to expect Me to show up in everything you do and everywhere you go so I can support you, endorse you, assist you, make things easier, provide you with advantages and grant special privileges."* You can read this statement in his book "Walking In Divine Favor."

"When favour is thrown into a story, by the Divine or man, it takes a new shape and meaning."

Frederick Osei-Manu

"The proof of favour is surprises."

Frederick Osei-Manu

About two years ago, I walked into a bookshop and saw an old man go through the various aisles. Being a lover of books myself, I walked to him and held a conversation with. We spoke for a while and covered so many subjects. During our conversation, I felt the need to give him free copies of books. So I quickly rushed to my car to pick the books for him. He later texted back in the day thanking me for my gesture and how much he enjoyed reading my book "The Life Coach Next Door."

Life is designed such that we keep running into people: be it friends, family and total strangers. It is mind-boggling when a stranger decides to help you even when you have not solicited for their help.

Again, there was a time back in London when I needed money to sort out certain bills. To my surprise, I received a tax refund from the Internal Revenue Service (IRS). I was not expecting this. I am sure I am not the only one who has experienced this. I believe it was the favour of God that made a way for me in that time of my need.

Anytime I think on this subject (out of the blue), Ruth comes to mind. This young lady follows Naomi to Israel not knowing what the future held for her. One day she tells her mother-in-law (Naomi) – *"I want to go out in the fields of Bethlehem to glean"*. She strangely goes to glean on the fields of Boaz.

Later in the day Boaz sees Ruth in the fields and asks his servants who she was. They tell him she is a stranger (Moabite lady who followed Naomi to town). Just the mere sighting of Ruth by Boaz made her highly favoured.

The Boaz spoke to Ruth: "Listen, my daughter. From now on don't go to any other field to glean - stay right here in this one. And stay close to my young women. Watch where they are harvesting and follow them. And don't worry about a thing; I've given orders to my servants not to harass you. When you get thirsty, feel free to go and drink from the water buckets that the servants have filled." She dropped to her knees, then bowed her face to the ground. "How

does this happen that you should pick me out and treat me so kindly –me, a foreigner. (Ruth 2:8-10, MSG)

As if this was not enough, as the conversation builds up something amazing takes place.

She said, "Oh sir, such grace, such kindness – I don't deserve it. You've touched my heart, treated me like one of your own. And I don't even belong here! At lunch break, Boaz said to her, "Come over here; eat some bread. Dip it in the wine." So she joined the harvesters. Boaz passed the roasted grain to her. She ate her fill and even had some left over. (Ruth 2:13-14, MSG)

From this episode, you would probably be thinking it is enough for the day. God had more surprises under his sleeves for Ruth. Now watch this.

...Boaz ordered his servants: "Let her glean where there's still plenty of grain on the ground – make it easy for her. Better yet, pull some of the good stuff out and leave it for her to glean. Give her special treatment." (Ruth 2:15-16, MSG)

Do you know what Ruth did not have from the beginning of the day, favour gave to her? Favour released much more than she could imagine and handle. I wonder what her night would be while she was reminiscing on the events of the day. Indeed, favour makes the outrageous to happen so fast that it "makes ones' head to spin". One event after another made this rich and prominent Boaz fall in love with Ruth and finally married her. I suggest you read the whole book of Ruth, it is lovely to do so.

End Note

Dr Jerry Savelle

Walking In Divine Favor, pg 87

Chapter 8

No Good Thing Will God Withhold

Behold, O God our shield, and look upon the face of thine anointed. For a day in thy courts is better than a thousand. I had rather be a doorkeeper in the house of my God, than to dwell in the tents of wickedness. For the LORD God is a sun and shield: the LORD will give grace and glory: no good thing will he withhold from them that walk uprightly. (Psalms 84:9-11)

When favour is at work, every door swings open effortlessly. Heaven and earth are compelled to not hold anything good back when one is walking in the favour of God. It is quite amazing to observe the ways of a favoured person; they turn to have a Midas touch on everything they do. Flourish is the buzzword and it sounds in the background of a person experiencing the realities of favour.

It is not surprising to see from the scripture that grace (favour) and glory walk hand-in-hand. Glory is a realm of no struggles. What a way to live when everything is working perfectly and harmonious in favour of your cause in life! I am not saying challenges will not come but even when they do come, they tend to lift you up and make you a better person. This is what in Christian circles we refer to as *"everything is working for my good."*

When a person decides not to withhold a thing from another it means such a person is in a good position to give out his or her goods to anyone who is willing to receive. With this understanding, we know God is never in a bad mood but always in a good mood and wants to give his best goods to us.

If a son shall ask bread of any of you that is a father, will he give him a stone? or if he ask a fish, will he for a fish give him a serpent? Or if he shall ask an egg, will he offer him a scorpion? If ye then, being evil [natural, earthly and mundane], know how to give good gifts unto your children: how much more shall your heavenly Father give the Holy Spirit to them that ask him? (Luke 11:11-13 with the author's

insertion)

You have to understand that when Jesus spoke in regard to Luke 11:11-13, he portrayed the common practice of fathers in the Orient or Eastern world. These fathers in question would always give the basic needs to their children by way of bread, fish and egg for their upkeep. We should then know that we are into something bigger when we come to God for his favour.

God is more than willing to give us good gifts- with the Holy Spirit as His first and best gift to all His children. The best capital a father can give to a son or daughter is not houses, cars, money etc. but their person. God says, *"I am willing to give all the earthly things to my sons and daughters but more than that- my own Spirit"*. When we receive the Holy Spirit, we have actually gained the greatest favour a man can ever ask or dream about getting from God.

Chapter 9

There Is Favour Awaiting Us At The Throne

Let us, therefore, come boldly unto the throne of grace, that we may obtain mercy, and find grace to help in time of need. (Hebrews 4:16)

So let's walk right up to him and get what he is so ready to give. Take the mercy, accept the help. (Hebrews 4:16, MSG)

Let us then fearlessly and confidently and boldly draw near to the throne of grace (the throne of God's unmerited favour to us sinners), that we may receive mercy [for our failures] and find grace to help in good time for every need [appropriate help and well-timed help, coming just when we need it]. (Hebrews 4:16, AMP)

When we come before the throne of God, two things happen to us: we receive mercy and grace (favour). Mercy cancels judgements (any wrong conclusions and failures in our lives) and favour gives us a fresh boost of help to move on in life.

So as a believer you must take great interest in spending time before God's throne. When God favours a man or woman it is greater than anything one can imagine. God intends that anytime we relate with Him we be conscious of His mercy and favour.

The Greek word for 'obtain' is 'lambano' which means to *catch, receive, accept* and *get hold of.* It is with this in mind that you say I receive God's favour on my life and I expect it to affect the people and the world around me. Favour actually makes the universe (time, space and time) to connive with us to bring us to our God-intended place in life.

It is C.S Lewis who said *"God has not chosen to write the whole of history with His own hand. Most of the events that go on in the universe are indeed out of our control, but not all."* In other words, once we obtain God's favour we are allowed to contribute with our time, talents and effort to make something special happen. So whether history or events under the sun is contrary to our expectations, we can change it by the power of favour.

I am yet to see a man who has no need. We all need love, goods (clothing, food, water, shelter and money), help etc. at diverse times. God wants to actively participate in our lives so He beckons us all the time to come for his free, prompt and well-tailored help.

Let me quickly bring this to your notice: at the throne, God releases angels to bring us special help. When God sends angelic help our way it does much more than our own calculated plans.

Behold, I send an Angel before thee, to keep thee in the way, and to bring thee into the place which I have prepared. (Exodus 23:20)

The Bible is full of accounts of how angels have played a role in people for them to reach their destinies. Let me mention a few here:

- Angels were released to protect the tree of life (see Genesis 3:24).
- An angel was at the burning bush when God called Moses (see Acts 7:30).
- Two angels and the Lord visited Abraham to announce the new season of laughter (i.e. the

birth of Isaac) to him and Sarah (see Genesis 18:1-3).

- In the den of lions, Daniel was kept alive because of the angels of God
- Hagar and Ishmael were preserved when they run out of water by an angel of the Lord (see Genesis 21:17-19).
- God sent an angel to Joseph to warn him of an impending danger. He took Mary and Jesus to Egypt for their safety (see Matthew 2:13).
- An angel announced the birth of Jesus to the shepherds in the field (see Luke 2:8-20).
- An angel told Zechariah that he and the wife would have a child of their own in their old age (see Luke 1:13).
- An angel was sent to stir the pool of Bethsaida to bring healing to the sick (see John 5:4).
- An angel of God brought Peter out of prison (see Acts 5:19)
- Paul was informed by an angel that the voyagers he was with will be safe but they would lose their ship (see Acts 27:23).

- An angel told Philip to journey between Jerusalem and Gaza for him to meet the Ethiopian Eunuch (see Acts 8:26).

Let me touch on another thing that takes place at the throne of God - we get God's eyes fixed on our lives. It is Dr Mike Murdock who said, *"Those who see you determine the favour that comes toward you. And nobody receives favour unless he is seen."* When God takes notice of you, the world is obliged to look on you favourably.

It is true that the person who sees you can change your position in life. Let me prove this by looking at this scripture below.

WHEN JESUS SAW HIM lie, and knew that he had been now a long time in that case, he saith unto him, Wilt thou be made whole? (John 5:6)

This impotent man who was laid by the pool of Bethsaida for thirty-eight years got restored to normal life because Jesus looked on him. Many people saw him before Jesus did but they did not have the power to bring wholeness to him. When the right person

(Jesus) came along, the day of sorrows and pain was over in this man's life.

While closing this chapter, I felt moved by the Holy Spirit to touch on two extra things – faith and the voice of God.

But without faith it is impossible to please him: for he that cometh to God must believe that he is, and that he is a rewarder of them that diligently seek him. (Hebrews 11:6)

When one comes to God, he or she must believe that God is a 'Good Rewarder'. Without faith one is weak and impotent (or unable) to please and draw God's attention to oneself. We must believe who God says He is and will do. We must believe whatever He promised us in His word. Such confidence in God is what provokes his favour on our lives.

But he answered and said, It is written, Man shall not live by bread alone, but by every word that proceedeth out of the mouth of God. (Mark 4:4)

At the throne, we can dialogue with God. Just as a son or daughter can walk into the bedroom of the father or mother to hold a conversation; so it is when we come to the throne of our Heavenly Father. The same voice of God which brought everything into existence (heaven and earth) becomes expressly available to us. What can you not get done when you know you are backed by the voice of the Creator Himself? This is the beauty and reward of going daily to the very throne of God.

End Notes

C.S Lewis

The Collected Works Of C.S. Lewis, pg 371

Mike Murdock

The Assignment, pg 63

Chapter 10

The Master Cares

A land which the LORD thy God careth for: the eyes of the LORD thy God are always upon it, from the beginning of the year even unto the end of the year. (Deuteronomy 11:12)

In the 1980s, there were only a few Ghanaians who had sprinklers for their farms. One of my cousins' dad was privileged to own a number of these sprinklers. It made farming easier for him. Casting my mind back, my cousins had great produce from their farm year by year. What attributed to these excellent yields was the care given to these plants – of which the sprinkling of water was one of them. If a man can so much care for his plants, how much more will not God care for you.

God has got His eyes on you. Amazingly, throughout the year God's eyes are fixed on you. God never blinks His eyes nor does he slumber; so guess what, you are the picture He admires all day long.

Men May Decide Not To Care But God Cares

When my father and my mother forsake me, then the LORD will take me up. (Psalms 27:10)

For the LORD will not cast off his people, neither will he forsake his inheritance. (Psalms 94:14)

I always say men will always be men. When you are out of sight you are out mind. There are even times when one can be in sight and they will move to others. It is a curse to look on men as ones' source. My dealings with men have thought me that men can forget and disappoint you when their help is needed the most. Men are also limited to the kind of help they can even offer in the first place.

I prefer to go to God who cannot disappoint. You know what? God is not limited in any way as to what He can do. It is only God who can do the impossible. Actually, God makes the impossible possible. Read the following account for yourself and you will see how God really cares for us.

Then the eyes of the blind shall be opened, and the

ears of the deaf shall be unstopped. Then shall the lame man leap as an hart, and the tongue of the dumb [voiceless] sing: for in the wilderness shall waters break out, and streams in the desert. And the parched ground shall become a pool, and the thirsty land springs of water: in the habitation of dragons, where each lay, shall be grass with reeds and rushes. (Isaiah 35:5-7 with the author's insertion)

Cast Your Cares On God

Humble yourselves therefore under the mighty hand of God, that he may exalt you in due time: Casting all your care upon him; for he careth for you. (1 Peter 5:6, 7)

Take your burdens to God in your prayers. I have learnt that whenever I go to God to share my heart and mind on issues bothering me, by the time I am done I feel a weight lifted off me.

There are cares in your life you may find difficult to share with family and friends because of its weight and confidentiality. But with God, there is no problem too big to handle and when it comes to confidentiality, you are in safe hands.

Worry No More

Be careful for nothing; but in every thing by prayer and supplication with thanksgiving let your requests be made known unto God. And the peace of God, which passeth all understanding, shall keep your hearts and minds through Christ Jesus. (Philippians 4:6, 7)

We worry about so many things, even over things that do not exist. Our minds roam and we get disturbed with all the uncertainties around us. Worry compounds problems and makes them bigger than they originally were. I found that worry drains and sucks energy. Worry makes a man a weakling rather than a champion. When you worry, you do not have the power to change a day into night or vice versa. God does not want us to worry about anything. When a person worries, he or she is saying, *"I want to be in control of everything instead of God being in charge"*.

The solution Jesus gave them for worry is still relevant for the people of today.

So do not worry about tomorrow, for tomorrow will care for itself. Each day has enough trouble of its own. (Matthew 6:34, NASB)

Give your entire attention to what God is doing right now, and don't get worked up about may or may not happen tomorrow. God will help you deal with whatever hard things come up when the time comes. (Matthew 6:34, MSG)

In very intentional ways, decide to take one day at a time. Refuse to worry. When we free our souls from worry, we empower ourselves with the internal and invisible energy of God to accomplish the unimaginable.

It is Marcus Aurelius who said, *"never let the future disturb you, you will meet it, if you have to, with the same weapons of reason which today arm you against the present."* Often we worry about tomorrow or the future but get this in your spirit – God has got it all figured out. It is better we disturb not the serenity of our hearts, mind, body and the beauty of the future with our worries.

When we decide to pray to God over things that seem to bother our mind we soar above forces of worries that want to hold us down. Pray and sing your way into the victories God has for you on a daily basis.

Exhibit Patience Whiles God Comes Through

But let patience have her perfect work, that ye may be perfect and entire, wanting nothing. (James 1:4)

Going back and forth, pacing the floor in your corner about issues does not bring the answers we need. Patience is the greatest virtue one can exhibit whiles waiting for God to show Himself strong on his or her behalf.

God is all-seeing, all-knowing and all-good and is the One who has our lives and future in His hands; so it calls for us to exercise patience. Patience is a sure sign of our trust in God. By the virtue of patience, we wait on God and give Him room to do what He only does best – by miracles and favours.

Rugged Confidence That God Will Show You Favour

Cast not away, therefore, your confidence, which hath great recompense of reward. For ye have need of patience, that, after ye have done the will of God, ye might receive the promise. For yet a little while, and he that shall come will come, and will not tarry. Now the just shall live by faith: but if any man draw back, my soul shall have no pleasure in him. (Hebrews 10:35-38)

The three Hebrew boys who were thrown into the furnace of fire in the book of Daniel said whether God came through or not, they would trust Him. Eventually, they were delivered. This is rugged confidence in God. Whether good or bad, God is still who He is.

Let us remember that in a little while, God's favour will put us over and above any challenges we are faced with.

Chapter 11

Unforgettable Landmarks Of Success

In this chapter, I would like to share with you how favour got certain people to get landslide victories in life. These things I share are likely to also take place in your life, so read with an open heart. Let me set the ball rolling.

#1. Israel Gained The Promised Land By Favour

For they got not the land [of Canaan] in possession by their own sword, neither did their own arm save them; but Your right hand and Your arm and the light of Your countenance [did it], because You were favourable toward and did delight in them. You are my King, O God; command victories and deliverance for Jacob (Israel). (Psalms 44:3-4, AMP)

The nation Israel in their journey to possessing the Promised Land came into contact with nations that were military-wise stronger than them. So by human standards, Israel stood no chance in conquering these nations. But time and again we see in the book of Joshua how they overcame such might armies.

We discover in the scripture that there were three things that helped to secure Israel those victories- the right hand, arm and the light of God's face that made Israel, Israel.

#2. Samuel Became A Mighty & Recognised Prophet In Israel By Favour

Now the boy Samuel grew and was in favour both with the Lord and with men. (1 Samuel 2:26, AMP)

Samuel was a son of his mother's vow. His mother Hannah pledged to give him to God when she asked for a son from Him. God came to Samuel at a time when visions were rare in Israel. Twice God called him a little boy unto Himself.

Favour kept Samuel from following the evil ways of Eli's children. During his period under Eli's tutelage, God was raising for Himself a mighty prophet. It is a known fact from 'Dan to Beersheba' –

Samuel's words never dropped to the ground or without coming to pass. In other words, he was seasoned and inclined to the Spirit that when Samuel spoke it was like an oracle of God.

The boy Samuel who became a man was viewed and accepted as a revered prophet in Israel. When Samuel moved anywhere the people knew something significant would take place. This was the level of the prophetic operation in Samuel's life.

#3. Job's Greatness Began By Favour

You have granted me life and favour, and Your providence has preserved my spirit. (Job 10:12, AMP)

When you study the life of Job you will discover that he was a man of great wealth. He eventually lost everything. His large possessions, servants and children were lost in a day. What a calamity? Job came to ground-zero in his life. There was nothing to boast about at this time of his life. His health was even deteriorating; his wife suggested to him to curse God and die. His friends jumped into hasty conclusions that there was something he had done wrong.

However, Job knew something better. He knew that the one who had kept him alive would also favour him again. Amazingly the later days of Job were more glorious than when he was in his prime years.

So the LORD blessed the latter end of Job more than his beginning: for he had fourteen thousand sheep, and six thousand camels, and a thousand yoke of oxen, and a thousand she asses. He had also seven sons and three daughters. (Job 42:12-13)

#4. King David Took Notice Of What Favour Achieved For Him

For his anger endureth but a moment; in his favour is life: weeping may endure for a night, but joy cometh in the morning. And in my prosperity I said, I shall never be moved. LORD, by thy favour thou hast made my mountain to stand strong: thou didst hide thy face, and I was troubled. (Psalms 30:5-7)

Theologians or Bible scholars say David was born out

of wedlock. An outcast did not have a place among the legitimate children in Eastern culture. David was always relegated to the background. His destiny had been predetermined for him by no fault of his.

As a shepherd boy, he spent a greater part of his life in the bush. It is favour that made Saul's men recommend David to his service. It is the same favour that promoted David to prominence when he defeated Goliath. This same favour made Jonathan fall in love with him.

This same favour made him a captain over 400 hundred men in Adullam. This same favour made David and his men eat the showbread from God's altar without suffering death. This same favour kept him alive after all the plots of King Saul to alienate him. Favour was the mysterious strand woven in all of David journey before he finally became a king in Israel.

No wonder David was conscious of the favour of God on his life. He said God's favour is for a lifetime (see Psalms 30:5b). The favour of God got him the treasured possession in Israel — the throne. What else can this man ask for? He kept thanking God for establishing his reign by favour.

#5. What Favour Would Do For Any Man

Let them shout for joy, and be glad, that favour my righteous cause: yea, let them say continually, Let the LORD be magnified, which hath pleasure in the prosperity of his servant. And my tongue shall speak of thy righteousness and of thy praise all the day long. (Psalms 35:27-28)

The Psalmist is explicitly clear that anybody who favours a righteous cause will not go unrewarded. When you and I have widespread interest in contributing something by way of love, time, labour, money and resources to the advancement of the Kingdom of God, you make yourself an automatic company of the favour of God.

Anybody working under the climate of favour will have many reasons to shout for joy. Believe it or not, favour is an indefinable force that can transform a person in a twinkle of an eye. Favour can make people stop in their track to make them praise and magnify God for the great things He is doing for you. Just as by the means of light darkness disappears, so does favour make lack exit with force and ushers in ever-increasing prosperity. The truth is that favour will always make it such that you would have something good to talk about. What about that?

Chapter 12

Supernatural Crowning

For You are the glory of their strength [their proud adornment], and by Your favour our horn is exalted and we walk with uplifted faces! (Psalms 89:17, AMP)

To be crowned is to be honoured and dignified before men. Favour has a way of crowning people. When I see a person with a glowing face, I think of favour. Favour will bypass any human ability, education, background and culture to get you what you desire.

A well-decorated person usually comes from a wealthy family. Nonetheless, favour can adorn any man or woman and put them unto the highest stage in this life. So we know that favour is a decorator of men. When favour comes upon a person, it becomes a difference maker. Favour can cause one to move from little to plenty, from unknown to recognition, from poor to rich and more when favour is at work.

In recent times, when Prince William got married to his girlfriend Catherine Middleton, a lot of people across the world said this lady was fortunate to be part of the Royal Family of England. In a day, she ceased to be commoner to become the Duchess of Cambridge. Her crowning and wedding were hugely covered by the media. Tell me if this is not favour.

You observe that every crowning goes with the presentation of gifts. It is therefore not surprising that when one begins to walk in favour, people love to lavish gifts or parcels on them.

And the daughter of Tyre shall be there with a gift; even the rich among the people shall intreat thy favour. (Psalms 45:12)

I will never forget this experience I am about to share. I once walked into a clothing shop with my uncle and his son in the United States. I walk to the counter to pay for the clothing I had picked, my uncle steps in and tells the teller to bill him instead. If my memory serves me right, the amount was about $200.00. What have I done to deserve this act of favour? I was stunned. Some people have experienced this too in diverse ways. Some even have experienced something bigger than what happened to me. But the bottom-line is favour has the capacity to enrich a person's life.

This is all more surprising when you see how God crowned the nation of Israel with favour. Supernaturally, natural Israel became a super nation and obtained a rich status without any doing of theirs.

And it shall be, when the LORD thy God shall have brought thee into the land which he sware unto thy fathers, to Abraham, to Isaac, and to Jacob, to give thee great and goodly cities, which thou buildedst not, And houses full of all good things, which thou filledst not, and wells digged, which thou diggedst not, vineyards and olive trees, which thou plantedst not; when thou shalt have eaten and be full; Then beware lest thou forget the LORD, which brought thee forth out of the land of Egypt, from the house of bondage. (Deuteronomy 6:10-12)

It is again mind boggling to know that Israel did not have to work to gain the cities and great possessions they got. It is good to work for what we want but favour has the power to get us what we can hardly get by our own efforts.

Do you know when a person is crowned his or her security is beefed up or tightened? God always fortifies the life of His favoured ones. In reality, God is the buckler to these favoured ones.

For thou, LORD, wilt bless the righteous; with favour wilt thou compass him as with a shield. (Psalms 5:12)

Obviously, by now you have seen how favour works. Let me throw in a new thought here. Favour creates an atmosphere around a person. There is an atmosphere that makes things to flourish. Favour is compared to the latter rain (spring rain).

In the light of the king's countenance is life; and his favour is as a cloud of the latter rain. (Proverbs 16:15)

The latter rain (spring rain) is known to be responsible to make seeds or grains to swell before they finally come to maturity. It is a known fact the spring rains bring about the refreshing of seeds and the ripening of crops. A farmer in Israel usually looked up to this spring rain to see the blessing and prosperity of his fields. This rains normally come around March and April. So when we see the spring rains we can say harvest is around the corner. What a way to know you can be crowned with bumper harvest in your field. With all these happenings, it is like having the King of the Universe smile towards a man or woman having gained His favour.

End Notes

Wedding Of Prince William And Catherine Middleton
https://en.wikipedia.org/wiki/Wedding_of_Prince_William_and_Catherine_Middleton

Kate Middleton Biography - Biography
https://www.biography.com/people/kate-middleton-542648

Easton's Bible Dictionary – Rain
https://www.blueletterbible.org/search/Dictionary/viewTopic.cfm?topic=ET0003056,IT0007247,NT0004041,TT0000467,BT0003516

NETBible: Rain
http://classic.net.bible.org/dictionary.php?word=RAIN

Conclusion

[Earnestly] remember me, O Lord, when You favour Your people! O visit me also when You deliver them, and grant me Your salvation! - That I may see and share the welfare of Your chosen ones, that I may rejoice in the gladness of Your nation, that I may glory with Your heritage. (Psalms 106: 4-5, AMP)

We have really covered some ground concerning the subject of favour. Favour can be very fascinating. When the King comes visiting the neighbourhood, may He also come into your house. In that way, you bring yourself up to what God is doing. This is where you say you have been remembered.

I hear the sound of favour blow; may it swell, pull things in from different circles that may wreck the logic of the day. It may unsettle you but it is all the better because this will not destroy you but cause you to soar.

But God, being rich in mercy, because of the great love with which he loved us, even when we were dead in our trespasses, made us alive together with Christ - by grace you have been saved (Ephesians 2:4-5, ESV)

God is rich in mercy and also rich in favour. What is available to a father is expressly disposable to his sons and daughters. Of course, what God has is certainly yours for the taking. Think about this, it has always been the Father's interest and good pleasure to give us the Kingdom (see Luke 12:32).

Receiving and having Christ in one's heart and life is the highest form of favour a person can have. Most times people seek favour to get things but the One who made all things has put Himself on a silver platter for you to take. There is no price tag on salvation because if there was, no man could afford it. So I encourage you to embrace this gift of favour in the person of His son Jesus Christ that God has given to humanity.

Before I draw the curtains on this book, I want to drive home my last thoughts. Take a good look at yourself today because favour can change you in and out. Notice what the scripture below says:

And after you have suffered a little while, the GOD OF ALL GRACE, who has called you to his ETERNAL GLORY in CHRIST will himself

RESTORE, CONFIRM, STRENGTHEN, and ESTABLISH you. (1 Peter 5:10, ESV)

When favour meets or rubs on a person, the outcome afterwards is really incredible. Dr Mike Murdock said, *"One day of favour is worth a thousand days of labour."* Favour is known by the fruits it produces in the life of a person. At least there are four main things that will happen to the person who is highly favoured. Take a look at the list below:

- Favour will restore a person.
- Favour will confirm a person into his or her place.
- Favour will supernaturally strengthen any person it comes in contact with.
- Favour will establish you.

Finally, there is such rich truth in this book that I encourage you to share with others. Be blessed and see you at the top through the favour of God.

End Note

Mike Murdock

The Assignment, pg 63

Frederick Osei-Manu

www.ingramcontent.com/pod-product-compliance
Ingram Content Group UK Ltd.
Pitfield, Milton Keynes, MK11 3LW, UK
UKHW041935190726
13854UKWH00004B/1597